PRACTICING SELF-CARE

BY STEPHANIE FINNE

BLUE OWL
BOOKS

TIPS FOR CAREGIVERS

Social and emotional learning (SEL) helps children manage emotions, learn how to feel empathy, create and achieve goals, and make good decisions. Strong lessons and support in SEL will help children establish positive habits in communication, cooperation, and decision-making. By incorporating SEL in early reading, children will be better equipped to build confidence and foster positive peer networks.

BEFORE READING

Talk to the reader about self-care. Explain that it is more than just taking care of your body.

Discuss: What do you think self-care is? Why is self-care important?

AFTER READING

Talk to the reader about practicing self-care daily. Explain that it can be different based on what his or her mind or body needs each day.

Discuss: What activities make you feel calm? What do you do that makes you feel confident? Can these things be added to your daily routine to help your well-being?

SEL GOAL

Some students may struggle with recognizing or acknowledging what their minds and bodies need. Help readers develop self-care skills. Help them learn to stop and think about their feelings and body sensations. Sensations can be clues to finding out what they are feeling and what they need to manage those feelings. Discuss how learning to do these things can help them identify their physical, mental, and emotional needs.

TABLE OF CONTENTS

CHAPTER 1

WHAT IS SELF-CARE?

Are there things you do to care for yourself each day? Maybe you make sure to get enough sleep so you're not tired. Tia draws because it helps her feel **relaxed**.

Jackson finds happiness in cooking. These are all forms of **self-care**. Self-care can be doing an activity that feels good for your mind and body. Doing these types of activities helps your mind and body stay healthy.

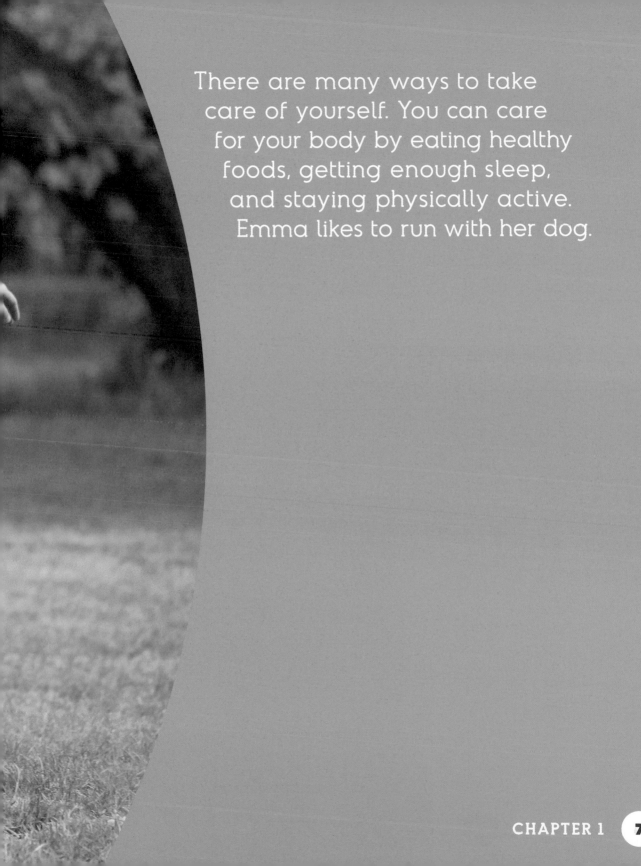

There are many ways to take care of yourself. You can care for your body by eating healthy foods, getting enough sleep, and staying physically active. Emma likes to run with her dog.

You can care for your **mental health** by being **mindful** of your feelings. **Identify** your feelings and body **sensations**. Sensations can be clues. They can help you find out what you are feeling. Mack talks with his dad about his feelings.

CHAPTER 2

HOW IT HELPS

What does **stress** feel like for you? Tyler's muscles get tight. He gets a headache and fuzzy thoughts. He closes his eyes and takes deep breaths to help. He is creating a healthy **habit**.

Limiting screen time also helps. One way is to practice "slow down" time. This is when there are no devices and everyone does a quiet activity. You may read, draw, **meditate**, or practice yoga.

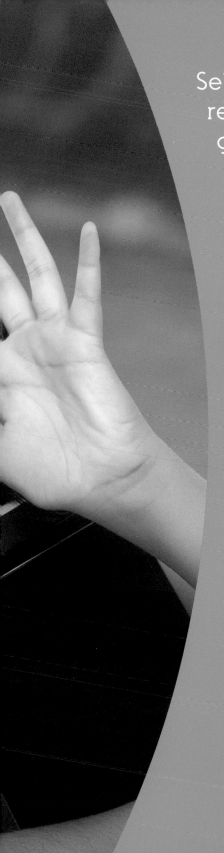

Self-care helps you succeed and reach your **goals**. Maybe your goal is to be happy and share that with others. You find that smiling helps, so you smile at others.

SMILE

When you smile, your brain releases **endorphins**. Even if you are not feeling happy, the act of smiling might help you get there! Find a joke that makes you laugh. Share it with a friend.

CHAPTER 3

STEPS TO SELF-CARE

Work self-care into your **routine**. First, identify how you deal with stress. Do you exercise? Maybe you talk to a friend. Make a list of the things you already do.

The second step is to find what else makes you feel good. Try being creative. Writing or drawing can help you work through your feelings. Mayim and her sister like to dance and make music.

The third step is to add the new activity to your routine. A routine gives you something to rely on. See where you can add the new activity into your day.

LOOK FOR PROBLEMS

Are there things that will stop you from adding the activity to your routine? Maybe you want to journal before school. But there isn't enough time. You may need to adjust your schedule.

The fifth step is to **commit**. Make a mindful decision to take care of yourself. You deserve it! When you take care of yourself, you feel happier. Then it is easier to be a good friend and **community** member.

VOLUNTEERING

Volunteering can be part of your self-care. You can help at a food shelf or write someone a kind note. Find a way of helping that connects you to others.

The sixth step is to share your plan with family and friends. They can **support** you. They might have suggestions to try. They might even join you!

Finally, follow through! Practice your self-care activities as often as possible. Track how it is going. How does it make you feel? What physical and mindful activities will you add to your daily routine?

GOALS AND TOOLS

GROW WITH GOALS

Self-care is a skill that takes a lot of practice. Try working these goals into your daily routine.

Goal: Make a list! List things that make you feel calm. Then make a list of times you can do these calming activities.

Goal: Talk to an adult you trust. He or she can help you think of activities to add to your self-care routine. Always ask for help if you need it.

Goal: Practice! Keep trying new things to see what makes you feel good. Add them to your daily routine.

TRY THIS!

Journaling can help you work through your thoughts and feelings. Bullet journaling is a way of writing in short lines. Make a line for each thought, task, event, or note. Make a symbol for each type of entry. Then get what is on your mind on paper. Track your mood each day. List your worries. Don't worry about putting things in a particular order or group. You can have fun with it by using different colored pens or by drawing pictures.

GLOSSARY

commit
To promise to do a specific thing or to support a specific cause.

community
A group of people who all have something in common.

endorphins
Substances created by the brain that reduce pain and cause pleasant feelings.

goals
Things you aim to do.

habit
An activity or behavior that you do regularly, often without thinking about it.

identify
To recognize or tell what something or who someone is.

meditate
To think deeply and quietly as a way of relaxing your mind and body.

mental health
The state of being mentally and emotionally sound.

mindful
A mentality achieved by focusing on the present moment and calmly recognizing and accepting your feelings, thoughts, and sensations.

relaxed
To feel less tense and at ease.

routine
A regular sequence of actions or way of doing things.

self-care
The practice of taking an active role in protecting one's own well-being and happiness, in particular during periods of stress.

sensations
Particular feelings that your body experiences.

stress
Mental or emotional strain, pressure, or worry.

support
To give help, comfort, or encouragement to someone or something.

TO LEARN MORE

FACT SURFER

Finding more information is as easy as 1, 2, 3.

1. Go to www.factsurfer.com

2. Enter "**practicingself-care**" into the search box.

3. Choose your book to see a list of websites.

INDEX

Blue Owl Books are published by Jump!, 5357 Penn Avenue South, Minneapolis, MN 55419, www.jumplibrary.com

Copyright © 2021 Jump! International copyright reserved in all countries. No part of this book may be reproduced in any form without written permission from the publisher.

Library of Congress Cataloging-in-Publication Data

Names: Finne, Stephanie, author.
Title: Practicing self-care / by Stephanie Finne.
Description: [Minneapolis]: Jump!, Inc., [2021] | Series: The sky's the limit | Includes index. | Audience: Grades: 2–3
Identifiers: LCCN 2020033339 (print) | LCCN 2020033340 (ebook)
ISBN 9781645278580 (hardcover)
ISBN 9781645278597 (paperback)
ISBN 9781645278603 (ebook)
Subjects: LCSH: Self-care, Health–Juvenile literature. | Mindfulness (Psychology)–Juvenile literature. | Well-being–Juvenile literature. | Mind and body–Juvenile literature.
Classification: LCC RA777 .F54 2021 (print) | LCC RA777 (ebook) | DDC 613–dc23
LC record available at https://lccn.loc.gov/2020033339
LC ebook record available at https://lccn.loc.gov/2020033340

Editor: Jenna Gleisner
Designer: Anna Peterson

Photo Credits: Nuiiko/Dreamstime, cover; poltu shyamal/Shutterstock, 1; bmf-foto.de/Shutterstock, 3; Nataliya Turpitko/Shutterstock, 4; miodrag ignjatovic/iStock, 5; VaLiza/Shutterstock, 6–7; Stock Rocket/Shutterstock, 8–9; Khosro/Shutterstock, 10; Asier Romero/Shutterstock, 11; Just dance/Shutterstock, 12–13 (left); Feverpitched/Dreamstime, 12–13 (right); igoriss/iStock, 14; Silverblack/Dreamstime, 15; KK Tan/Shutterstock, 16–17; SDI Productions/iStock, 18–19; Lacheev/Dreamstime, 20–21.

Printed in the United States of America at Corporate Graphics in North Mankato, Minnesota.